WITHDRAWN

Today's SUPERSTARS

Drew Brees

By Michael Portman, 1976-

 Gareth Stevens
Publishing

Please visit our Web site, www.garethstevens.com. For a free color catalog of all our high-quality books, call toll free 1-800-542-2595 or fax 1-877-542-2596.

Library of Congress Cataloging-in-Publication Data

Portman, Michael, 1976-
 Drew Brees / Michael Portman.
   p. cm. — (Today's superstars)
 Includes bibliographical references and index.
 ISBN 978-1-4339-3993-8 (pbk.)
 ISBN 978-1-4339-3994-5 (6-pack)
 ISBN 978-1-4339-3992-1 (library binding)
 1. Brees, Drew, 1979---Juvenile literature. 2. Football players—United States—Biography—Juvenile literature. 3. Quarterbacks (Football)—United States—Biography—Juvenile literature. 4. New Orleans Saints (Football team)—Juvenile literature. I. Title.
 GV939.B695P67 2011
 796.332092--dc22
 [B]
                                    2010011662

First Edition

Published in 2011 by
Gareth Stevens Publishing
111 East 14th Street, Suite 349
New York, NY 10003

Copyright © 2011 Gareth Stevens Publishing

Designer: Christopher Logan
Editor: Therese Shea

Photo credits: Cover, p. 1 Chris McGrath/Getty Images; pp. 4–5, 12 Andy Lyons/Getty Images; pp. 6, 7, 28, 30 Chris Graythen/Getty Images; pp. 8, 19 Al Messerschmidt/Getty Images; p. 9 Win McNamee/Getty Images; p. 10 Harry How/Allsport/Getty Images; p. 13 Shutterstock.com; p. 14 Larry French/Getty Images; p. 15 Joe Raedle/Newsmakers/Getty Images; pp. 16–17, 20 Stephen Dunn/Allsport/Getty Images; pp. 18, 41, 46 Jonathan Daniel/Allsport/Getty Images; p. 21 Bill Frakes/Sports Illustrated/Getty Images; pp. 22–23, 27, 44 Donald Miralle/Getty Images; p. 24 David Maxwell/Getty Images; p. 25 Ronald Martinez/Getty Images; p. 26 Joe Robbins/Getty Images; p. 31 Jeff Gross/Getty Images; p. 33 Doug Benc/Getty Images; p. 34 Frederick M. Brown/Getty Images; p. 36 Chris Graythen/NBAE via Getty Images; p. 37 Skip Bolen/Getty Images; p. 38 Greg Nelson/Sports Illustrated/Getty Images; p. 39 Steve Grayson/Getty Images; p. 40 Brandon Lopez/Allsport/Getty Images.

Printed in the United States of America

CPSIA compliance information: Batch #CS10GS: For further information contact Gareth Stevens, New York, New York at 1-800-542-2595.

Contents

Words in the glossary appear in **bold** type the first time they are used in the text.

"We just believed in ourselves and we knew that we had an entire city

AND MAYBE AN ENTIRE COUNTRY BEHIND US."

—Drew Brees

Brees takes aim in Super Bowl XLIV on February 7, 2010.

Chapter 1

Super Saints

February 7, 2010. Super **Bowl** XLIV (44). The Indianapolis Colts were ahead 17–16 with just under 6 minutes to play. Drew Brees knew the New Orleans Saints had to work quickly. The Saints had the ball at the 2-yard line. Brees got the ball, took a step back, and fired off a short pass to Jeremy Shockey in the end zone. The Saints grabbed the lead, 22–17. Rather than kick for an extra point, the Saints took a gamble. They went for a **two-point conversion**. The pass from Brees was caught by Lance Moore in the end zone. The Saints were up by 7 points.

The game wasn't over yet. The Colts still had time to tie the game with a touchdown. The Saints' defense had to make sure that didn't happen.

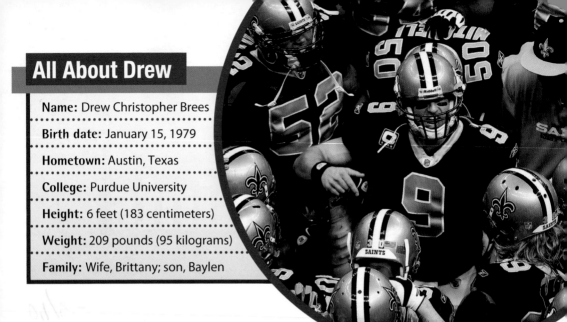

As a quarterback, Drew Brees is the leader of his team.

Fact File

The New Orleans Saints won their first playoff game in 33 years in 2000.

Just a Dream

The Super Bowl had been just a dream for the New Orleans Saints for most of their 43-year history. There had been a few good teams over the years, but not many people took them seriously.

In 2006 — Brees's first season with the Saints — he took them to the playoffs. By the beginning of the 2009 season, the Saints were confident they could be a championship team. "I think it's the best team we've had since I've been here," Brees said.

On a Roll

In 2009, the Saints kept finding ways to win. An undefeated season seemed possible, but they lost their final three games. However, it didn't matter. The Saints had made it to the playoffs.

The **division** playoff game ended in a 45–14 win over the Arizona Cardinals. The National Football Conference (NFC) Championship game against the Minnesota Vikings wasn't so easy. Still, the Saints won in **overtime** with a **field goal**. The New Orleans Saints were going to their first Super Bowl!

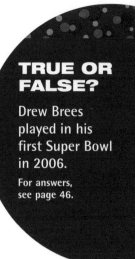

TRUE OR FALSE?

Drew Brees played in his first Super Bowl in 2006.

For answers, see page 46.

Head coach Sean Payton hugs Brees after the Saints win the NFC Championship.

7

Welcome to Miami

Brees and the Saints knew it would be a challenge playing the Indianapolis Colts in Super Bowl XLIV. The Colts quarterback, Peyton Manning, is considered one of the best quarterbacks of all time. The Saints would have to play their best if they hoped to win. "It's a moment I've been waiting for, for a very long time," Brees said, "and obviously we're not done yet." The team headed to Miami, Florida, the chosen site for Super Bowl XLIV.

Archie Manning

Friendly Rivals

Peyton Manning's father, Archie, was a quarterback for the Saints in the 1970s and 1980s. Archie is very popular in the city of New Orleans. He's involved in helping the community, including raising money to rebuild parts of New Orleans after Hurricane Katrina.

Drew and Archie live close to each other in New Orleans. They've become good friends. If Peyton's Colts hadn't been in the Super Bowl, Archie would have been cheering for Brees and the Saints.

Go Saints Go!

Many people expected the Colts to win Super Bowl XLIV, so it wasn't surprising when they grabbed an early lead. The Saints weren't about to give up, though. In the fourth quarter, they had a 7-point lead. Just when it looked like the Colts would tie the game, Tracy Porter **intercepted** a pass for the Saints and ran 74 yards for a touchdown. That was all it took—the Saints won, 31–17.

Drew Brees had proven that he was one of the best quarterbacks in the National Football League (NFL). After the game, he was named Super Bowl Most Valuable Player (MVP).

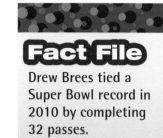

Fact File

Drew Brees tied a Super Bowl record in 2010 by completing 32 passes.

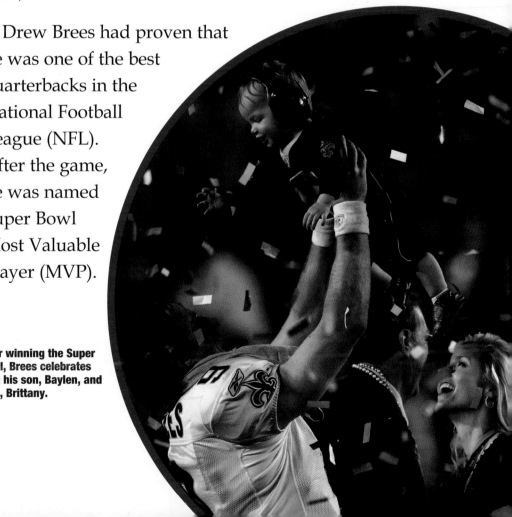

After winning the Super Bowl, Brees celebrates with his son, Baylen, and wife, Brittany.

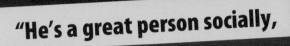

"He's a great person socially,

ATHLETICALLY, AND ACADEMICALLY."

—Greg Olson, Brees's college quarterbacks coach

Purdue quarterback Drew Brees looks for an open receiver in a game against Notre Dame on September 11, 1999.

Chapter 2

A Good Sport

Drew Christopher Brees was born on January 15, 1979, in Dallas, Texas. He seemed destined to become a professional athlete. His parents, Chip and Mina, were talented athletes in school. They named their son after Drew Pearson, a star **receiver** for the Dallas Cowboys. Drew's grandfather, Ray Akins, was one of the most successful high school football coaches in Texas. He had also been a soldier in World War II. Drew learned a lot about hard work and sacrifice from Ray.

When Drew was 7 years old, his family moved to Austin, Texas. Drew and his younger brother, Reid, often visited their grandparents on their Texas ranch. Those visits were an important part of growing up for Drew.

Child's Play

▲ Brees celebrates a
touchdown pass in
Super Bowl XLIV.

**TRUE OR
FALSE?**

Brees throws with
his left hand.

Drew enjoyed the time he and Reid
spent at the ranch. "They were rowdy
little boys who liked to play," their
grandmother said, "but they were good
boys." Their grandfather, Ray, also kept
the boys busy with chores. It was hard
work, but Drew enjoyed it.

Sometimes, Ray would bring the boys
with him to football practices. Drew and
Reid would run around on the sidelines
or play catch. For a young boy, throwing
a full-sized football wasn't easy!

Starting Out

Brees played football in middle school. The school he attended didn't have tackle football. They played flag football instead. It wasn't how most Texas kids got their start, but Brees credits those games with helping him to become a better quarterback. "You're throwing the ball on every play," he said. "I think you're just able to develop a lot faster."

Fact File

Brees was born with a large birthmark on his right cheek. His parents decided not to have it removed.

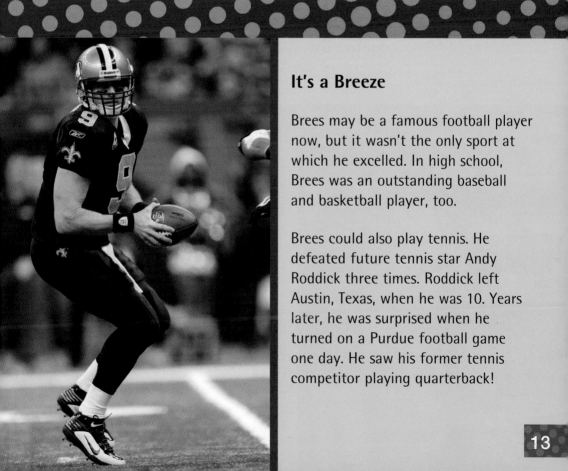

It's a Breeze

Brees may be a famous football player now, but it wasn't the only sport at which he excelled. In high school, Brees was an outstanding baseball and basketball player, too.

Brees could also play tennis. He defeated future tennis star Andy Roddick three times. Roddick left Austin, Texas, when he was 10. Years later, he was surprised when he turned on a Purdue football game one day. He saw his former tennis competitor playing quarterback!

13

Opportunity Knocks

In 1993, Brees decided to go to Westlake High School. He joined the freshman football team. He guided that team to an undefeated season. Brees was the backup quarterback for the junior varsity team the next year. He wondered if he'd ever get to play. Brees told his mother, "I might want to quit football, just because I don't think I'm ever going to get an opportunity."

Just before the season began, the starting quarterback hurt his knee. Suddenly, Brees was the starter. The following year, he became the starting quarterback on the varsity team.

Fact File

Drew Brees's childhood nickname was "Cool Brees."

Standing Tall

At 6 feet (183 cm) tall, Drew Brees is considered short for an NFL quarterback. The average height of an NFL quarterback is 6 feet 3 inches (191 cm) tall. Many people believe that it's easier for a taller quarterback to scan the field and harder for defenders to block his passes. That means a shorter quarterback will often have to scramble, or run, to get a better view of the field. Drew has shown that a shorter quarterback can be successful.

A Serious Game

In Texas, no other sport is taken quite as seriously as football. Many high school teams play in large stadiums where each game can draw thousands of fans. Some of the biggest stars in college and the NFL got their start playing high school football in Texas.

School Days

Brees's final season at Westlake High was record breaking. The team finished with 16 wins and no losses. They won the state championship. Brees never lost a varsity game in which he started.

Despite Brees's success, **recruiters** were concerned that he was too small to play at the college level. Another worry was a knee injury at the end of his junior season. Only Kentucky and Purdue offered him **scholarships**. The Kentucky Wildcats already had Tim Couch, a star quarterback and **Heisman Trophy** contender. Brees had a better chance to play if he went to Purdue.

Fact File

In high school, Brees played on the basketball team with future NBA player Chris Mihm.

"We got lucky.

COLLEGE RECRUITING IS NOT AN EXACT SCIENCE."

—Purdue head coach Joe Tiller

Brees gets ready to pass at the Rose Bowl on January 1, 2001.

Chapter 3

College Game Day

A college quarterback's first season is always a learning experience. Compared to high school, the players are bigger, faster, and stronger. A quarterback has to be able to remain calm under pressure. When the defense is closing in, it's not enough to have a strong arm. If a quarterback gets nervous and makes the wrong decisions, he'll lose games. Brees has always been known to remain calm and make the right decisions.

Brees didn't see much action during his first season as a Purdue Boilermaker. However, he spent hours learning plays and studying the opposing defenses. By the start of his second season, Brees was eager to prove himself on the field.

Remember the Alamo Bowl

Purdue Boilermakers football had been struggling for many years. Brees mostly watched from the sidelines during his freshman year as Purdue completed a long-awaited winning season. In 1998, he got his chance to be the starting quarterback. He was going to do his best to make sure they kept on winning.

With Drew Brees leading them, the Boilermakers once again had a winning season, with nine wins and four losses. Brees's play earned him the title of **Big Ten** Player of the Year. For the second straight year, Purdue ended their season with a victory in the Alamo Bowl, this time over Kansas State. Few had expected Purdue to beat the fourth-best team in the country.

Brees runs to get in a better position to pass the ball in a 1999 Purdue game.

Decisions, Decisions

In the 2000 Outback Bowl, Purdue had an early lead, 19–0. The Georgia Bulldogs battled back. Brees's remarkable passes weren't enough. Georgia won in overtime, 28–25.

Despite the loss, Brees showed that he was one of the best quarterbacks in college. He finished fourth in the Heisman Trophy voting. He considered skipping his senior year to enter the NFL **draft**. However, Brees had gotten to know NFL quarterback Peyton Manning. Manning advised him to finish his final season at Purdue.

Fact File
Brees graduated from Purdue University with a degree in industrial management and manufacturing.

What's a Boilermaker?

A boilermaker is a person who builds or repairs metal structures. It's difficult work. In 1891, a reporter used the term to describe the toughness of Purdue's football team. Because of their parents' professions, Purdue athletes were given nicknames such as pumpkin-shuckers, railsplitters, cornfield sailors, and blacksmiths. Boilermakers was the nickname that stuck.

Smelling the Roses

When Brees arrived at Purdue in 1997, many fans were unsure of his abilities. By 2000, it was a different story. That year, Brees led Purdue to a Big Ten championship as well as the school's first trip to the Rose Bowl since 1967. Brees threw two touchdowns, but the Washington Huskies won the game. Brees wasn't happy about the way the season ended, but he was proud of his second Big Ten Player of the Year award.

▼ Brees calls a play in a game against the Washington Huskies.

NFL Bound

When it came time for the 2001 NFL draft, many people thought Brees would be selected in the first round. However, like the college recruiters, NFL recruiters were worried about his small size. The first round came and went without a team choosing Brees.

The San Diego Chargers had the first pick in each round because of their losing 1–15 record the previous season. At the start of the second round, they decided to take a chance on Brees.

Fact File

Brees was featured on the cover of SEGA's 1999 NCAA College Football 2K2 video game.

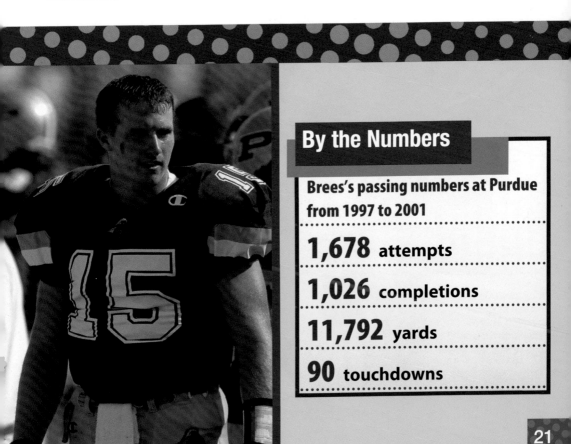

By the Numbers

Brees's passing numbers at Purdue from 1997 to 2001

1,678 attempts

1,026 completions

11,792 yards

90 touchdowns

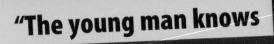

"The young man knows

HOW TO WIN."

—NFL coach Marty Schottenheimer

Brees protects the
football as Casey
Hampton of the
Pittsburgh Steelers
tries to take him down.

Chapter 4

California Dreaming

Brees faced a situation in San Diego similar to the one he had faced at Purdue. The Chargers were a struggling football team. They had finished last in their division three times in the previous 4 years. San Diego's first pick in the 2001 draft was running back LaDainian Tomlinson. Like Brees, Tomlinson was a high school football star in Texas. At a Heisman Trophy banquet the year before, Brees and Tomlinson had joked that it would be great if they could play on the same team. Now they were!

Both players wanted to do their part to make the Chargers a winning team. Tomlinson became the big story in San Diego that year. Brees, however, had to watch from the sidelines.

Flutie Effect

The Chargers' starting quarterback was Doug Flutie, a Heisman Trophy winner who had played in both the NFL and the Canadian Football League (CFL). After three seasons with the Buffalo Bills, he signed with San Diego. Although Brees played in only one game his first year, he was greatly influenced by Flutie's drive to win.

Early in the season, things looked sunny for San Diego, but the clouds soon rolled in. After losing their last nine games, the Chargers finished last in their division.

▼ Flutie and Brees discuss the San Diego game plan against the Cleveland Browns in 2003.

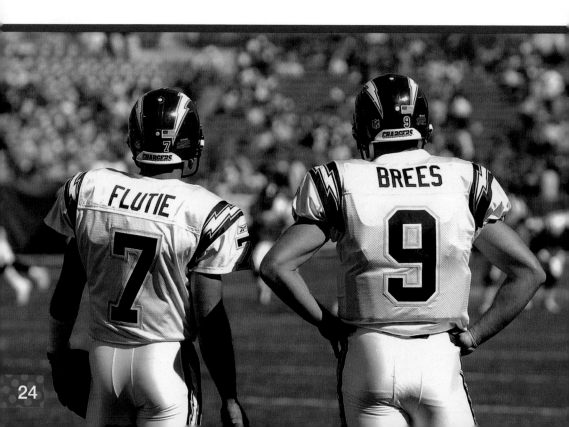

Starting and Stopping

Marty Schottenheimer was hired to coach the Chargers in 2002. He was impressed with Brees's skill and hard work during **training camp**. He decided to make Brees the starter. Brees played well that season, leading his team to an 8–8 record. However, San Diego missed the playoffs.

In the 2003 season, things didn't click between Brees and the Chargers. San Diego lost their first five games. Brees found himself on the sidelines, while Doug Flutie took the field.

Fact File

In a 2003 game against the Oakland Raiders, LaDainian Tomlinson threw a 21-yard touchdown pass to Drew Brees. It was Brees's first NFL touchdown catch.

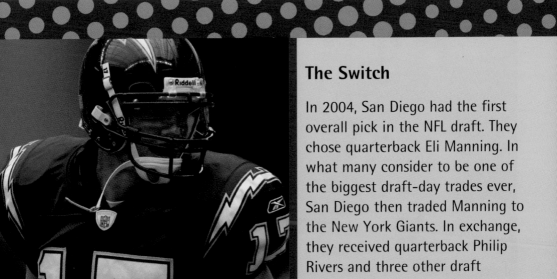

Philip Rivers

The Switch

In 2004, San Diego had the first overall pick in the NFL draft. They chose quarterback Eli Manning. In what many consider to be one of the biggest draft-day trades ever, San Diego then traded Manning to the New York Giants. In exchange, they received quarterback Philip Rivers and three other draft choices. The addition of Rivers was a sign that San Diego wasn't confident in Brees's future.

Comeback Kid

Brees knew that the 2004 season could be his most important. If he performed poorly, his chances of remaining a starting quarterback in the NFL were slim. He had thrown too many interceptions. He needed to find a way to throw more accurately.

After each practice, Brees stayed on the field and threw passes to a receiver. He often threw these passes with his eyes closed. Brees said, "It's taught me that even if you can't see, that doesn't mean you don't still have vision." Brees's vision guided his team to a 12–4 record. He earned the title of NFL Comeback Player of the Year in 2004.

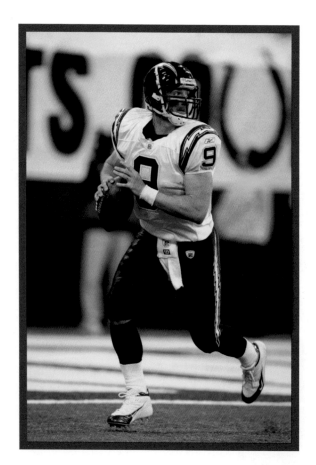

Brees was chosen for the Pro Bowl, the NFL all-star game, for the first time in 2004.

Time to Bolt

After the 2004 season, Brees became a **free agent**. He could have gone to another team, but the Chargers wanted him back for another year. Brees agreed. The 2005 season was a turning point in Brees's career. In the final game of the season, Brees suffered a shoulder injury to his throwing arm that required surgery.

Brees worked hard to get his arm back into shape. He was confident that he would be ready for the 2006 season. The Chargers weren't so sure. They wanted Philip Rivers to start. After getting offers from other teams, Brees decided to play for the New Orleans Saints.

TRUE OR FALSE?
Drew Brees has worn number 9 on his jersey since college.

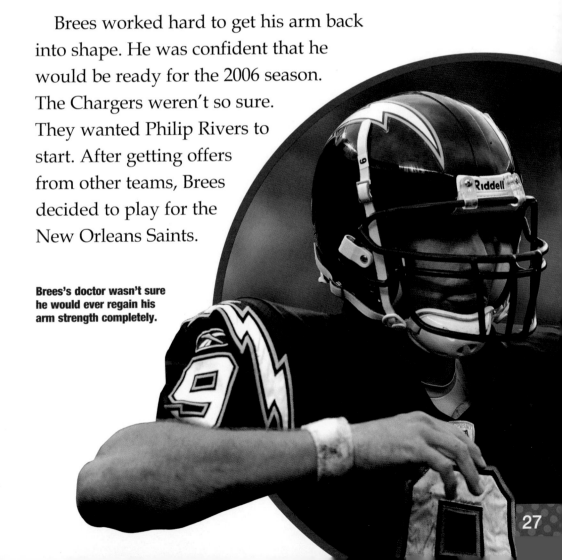

Brees's doctor wasn't sure he would ever regain his arm strength completely.

"HE'S SOMETHING ELSE!"

—Saints head coach Sean Payton

Brees runs out onto the field of the Superdome in a game against the New York Jets in 2009.

Chapter 5
Cool Brees in the Big Easy

After 2005's Hurricane Katrina, the city of New Orleans, Louisiana, was in bad shape. Homes and buildings had been destroyed. Countless people and businesses had left the city. The Saints' home, the Superdome, was badly damaged. While it was being repaired, the Saints played their 2005 home games in different cities.

By 2006, the city—often called the Big Easy—had begun the difficult process of rebuilding. The Superdome had been repaired and was ready to host games. In addition to Brees, the Saints had hired a new head coach, Sean Payton. They had also signed **running back** and Heisman Trophy winner Reggie Bush.

Return to the Superdome

On September 25, 2006, people across the United States tuned in to watch the Saints play their first game in the reopened Superdome. The Saints had won their first two away games. They took their home field against their longtime rivals, the Atlanta Falcons. "I never in my life heard a roar so loud," said the Falcons quarterback afterwards.

The Saints dominated the game, 23–3. Brees and his new team were giving the city a reason to cheer again.

▼ Saints fans enter the Superdome before a game against the Atlanta Falcons on November 2, 2009.

Proud City

Since their first season in 1967, the New Orleans Saints had a history of terrible teams. It took 21 years before they played a season in which they won more games than they lost.

In 2006, the Saints brought excitement and pride to the city of New Orleans. Brees took the team all the way to the NFC Championship for the first time in their history. Even though they lost to the Chicago Bears, the fans were still proud of the Saints.

TRUE OR FALSE?

In 2007, Brees's 440 completed passes set the NFL single-season record.

Bull's-Eye!

Could it be possible that Brees is more accurate than an Olympic archer? Some people might have a hard time believing it. In April 2009, the television program *Sport Science* put Brees to the test. The Olympic archers on the show hit a bull's-eye less than half the time. Brees hit a bull's-eye with a football ten out of ten times!

Numbers Game

The Saints had their ups and downs in the 2007 and 2008 seasons. They missed the playoffs both years. However, Brees kept playing well. In 2008, he became only the second quarterback in NFL history to throw for more than 5,000 yards in a single season! The Saints and their fans knew they had a good team. They hoped it wouldn't be long before they were in the playoffs again.

By the Numbers — Brees's passing numbers in the NFL

2001 San Diego: Completions: 15; Yards: 221; Touchdowns: 1

2002 San Diego: Completions: 320; Yards: 3,284; Touchdowns: 17

2003 San Diego: Completions: 205; Yards: 2,108; Touchdowns: 11

2004 San Diego: Completions: 262; Yards: 3,159; Touchdowns: 27

2005 San Diego: Completions: 323; Yards: 3,576; Touchdowns: 24

2006 New Orleans: Completions: 356; Yards: 4,418; Touchdowns: 26

2007 New Orleans: Completions: 440; Yards: 4,423; Touchdowns: 28

2008 New Orleans: Completions: 413; Yards: 5,069; Touchdowns: 34

2009 New Orleans: Completions: 363; Yards: 4,388; Touchdowns: 34

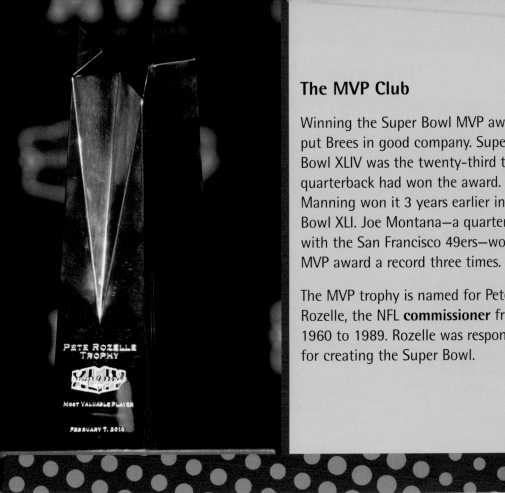

The MVP Club

Winning the Super Bowl MVP award put Brees in good company. Super Bowl XLIV was the twenty-third time a quarterback had won the award. Peyton Manning won it 3 years earlier in Super Bowl XLI. Joe Montana—a quarterback with the San Francisco 49ers—won the MVP award a record three times.

The MVP trophy is named for Pete Rozelle, the NFL **commissioner** from 1960 to 1989. Rozelle was responsible for creating the Super Bowl.

PETE ROZELLE
TROPHY

Most Valuable Player

February 7, 2010

The Saints Go Marching

In 2009, the Saints marched their way to a 13–3 regular season record. They continued with three wins in the playoffs. In Super Bowl XLIV, Brees had a nearly flawless performance. He threw for 288 yards and two touchdowns. The Saints' victory may have surprised some people, but not Brees. "I'm just feeling like it was all meant to be," the MVP said afterwards.

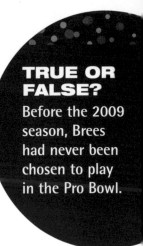

TRUE OR FALSE?
Before the 2009 season, Brees had never been chosen to play in the Pro Bowl.

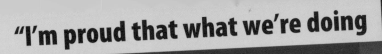

"I'm proud that what we're doing IS REALLY MAKING A DIFFERENCE."

—Drew Brees

Drew and Brittany Brees arrive at an awards ceremony in 2007.

Chapter 6

Off the Field

Drew Brees has always believed that actions speak louder than words. Throughout his career, questions have arisen about his size, speed, arm strength, and injuries. Brees has preferred to answer them with his performance on the field.

Brees takes the same approach off the field. He remembers being a little kid with big dreams. He's made it a goal to help others achieve their dreams. In 2003, when he was with the Chargers, Brees and his wife, Brittany, founded the Brees Dream Foundation. The foundation provides money for cancer research and is dedicated to improving life for people in need. "It's important to us," Brees said. "We care." Brees keeps showing that he cares—a lot.

Daring to Dream

When Brees arrived in New Orleans, the city was just starting its struggle to clean up after Hurricane Katrina. Brees and his foundation got to work raising money to rebuild schools, parks, playgrounds, and athletic fields.

Brees takes an active role and isn't afraid to get his hands dirty. "My wife, Brittany, and I have always been very hands-on with our foundation," he said.

Brees helps children learn important football skills at a camp in 2006.

Feel the Love

Drew and Brittany have embraced the city of New Orleans, and the city has returned that love. They bought a house in the city where they're raising their son, Baylen. They can often be seen eating in local restaurants and visiting local shops. Drew and Brittany are proud to call New Orleans home. According to fellow resident Archie Manning, "Drew and Brittany have been a great addition to the city."

Fact File

The Brees Dream Foundation has raised over $4 million for various causes.

▼ Brees enjoys the Super Bowl victory parade for the New Orleans Saints in 2010.

Staying Sharp

Brees knows that it takes hard work to be successful. Every effort counts. Brees spends long hours in the gym in order to stay in shape. The changes he's made to his diet have given him more energy and more strength. He doesn't just exercise his body. He also exercises his mind. He makes sure to visualize every play that a defense may try. He wants to be prepared for anything.

Brees's workout routine is hard work, but it pays off on the field.

Fun Facts

Drew's good-luck charm is a bracelet that says "Finish Strong."

Drew listens to music from the 1980s when he works out.

Drew loves root beer but will only drink it during the off-season.

Drew's favorite breakfast is peanut butter on toast with honey and banana.

▲ Brees takes time out of his football routine to focus on golf. Here he tees off at a 2004 golf tournament in Bermuda Dunes, California.

A Bright Future

Drew Brees has accomplished a lot in his career, both as a college player and a pro. He gave the city of New Orleans a reason to cheer after the tragedy of Hurricane Katrina.

Brees has worked hard to become the respected leader of a championship team. When talking about New Orleans, Brees says, "The city is on its way to recovery and in a lot of ways has come back better than ever." In a way, the same can be said of Drew Brees.

Fact File

Brees wants his son to learn to play golf because it's something he can always play. Football is too physically demanding for older people to play.

Timeline

1979 Drew Christopher Brees is born on January 15 in Dallas, Texas.

1996 Brees leads his high school football team to a 16–0 season and a state championship.

2000 Brees leads the Purdue Boilermakers to a Big Ten Championship.

2001 Brees is drafted by the San Diego Chargers.

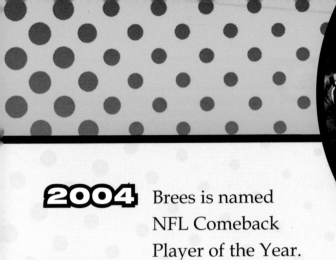

2004 Brees is named
NFL Comeback
Player of the Year.

....

2005 Hurricane Katrina hits
New Orleans, Louisiana.

....

2006 Brees leads the New Orleans
Saints to the playoffs in his
first year with the team.

....

2008 Brees throws for 5,069 yards,
just short of Dan Marino's
single-season record.

....

2010 Brees is named MVP of
Super Bowl XLIV.

....

Glossary

Big Ten: a group of college teams located mostly in the midwestern United States

bowl: a postseason game played between high-ranking football teams

commissioner: the head of a professional sport

division: a group of teams, usually located close to each other

draft: the selection of new players for a team

field goal: a kick that passes through a goal post, earning the kicking team three points

free agent: a player whose contract has ended, allowing him to sign a contract with a new team

Heisman Trophy: an award presented to the college football player voted the best in the country

intercept: to catch a pass thrown by the other team

overtime: the extra period played when the score is tied after regular play

receiver: an offensive player who catches passes

recruiter: someone who searches for people with great skills in a sport in order to add talent to a team

running back: an offensive player whose main job is to run with the ball but who can also catch passes

scholarship: money awarded to a student to pay for his or her education

training camp: the time before the season starts when players practice their skills

two-point conversion: when a team that has just scored a touchdown carries the ball across the goal line rather than kicking it and earns two points instead of one

To Find Out More

Books

Dougherty, Terri. *The Greatest Football Records.* Mankato, MN: Capstone Press, 2009.

Gitlin, Martin. *Football Skills: How to Play Like a Pro.* Berkeley Heights, NJ: Enslow Elementary, 2009.

Jacobs, Greg. *The Everything Kids' Football Book.* Avon, MA: Adams Media, 2010.

Magazines

Sports Illustrated and *Sports Illustrated Kids*
Read current news about Drew Brees and the Saints.

Web Sites

The Brees Dream Foundation
www.drewbrees.com
Read about Drew Brees and the Brees Dream Foundation.

Drew Brees
www.pro-football-reference.com/players/B/BreeDr00.htm
This site includes Brees's statistics in college and the NFL.

Drew Brees: Biography
www.jockbio.com/Bios/Brees/Brees_bio.html
Read a biography, facts, statistics, and what people say about Brees.

New Orleans Saints: Drew Brees
www.nfl.com/players/drewbrees/profile?id=BRE229498
See all of Brees's statistics since he joined the NFL.

Championships and Awards *

Big Ten Player of the Year
1998, 2000

Academic All-American Player of the Year
2000

Maxwell Award**
2000

NFL Comeback Player of the Year
2004

Pro Bowl Selection
2004, 2006, 2008, 2009

NFC Offensive Player of the Year
2006, 2008, 2009

Bert Bell Award***
2009

Super Bowl MVP
2010

*As of April 2010.

**An award given to the top
college football player, as voted
by sportscasters, sportswriters, and
coaches.

***An award given to the top pro football
players, as voted by NFL coaching staff,
writers, and reporters.

Source Notes

p. 4 Associated Press, "Brees Named Super Bowl MVP," Fox Sports, February 8, 2010, http://msn. foxsports.com/nfl/story/new-orleans-saints-drew-brees-named-super-bowl-xliv-mvp.

p. 6 Ed Staton, "Drew Brees Interview," BayouBuzz, 2009, http://www. bayoubuzz.com/News/Business/ Louisiana_Sports__New_Orleans_ Saints_Drew_Brees_Interview_ LSU_Hornets__9504.asp.

p. 8 Barry Wilner, "Saints Beat Vikings in OT, Reach 1st Super Bowl," Nola.com, January 25, 2010, http://stats.nola.com/fb/recap.as p?g=2010124018&home=18&vis= 16&final=true.

p. 10 Gwenn Miller, "Mark of a Winner," *The Daily Collegian*, September 30, 2000, http:// www.collegian.psu.edu/ archive/2000/09/09-30-00cm/ 09-30-00cm-5.asp,.

p. 12 Miller.

p. 13 Juan Kincaid, "Brees Overcame Hurdles on Way to NFL Stardom," WWLTV.com, November 9, 2009, http://www.wwltv. com/news/slideshows/ wwl110309cbdawgy-69032362. html.

p. 14 Kincaid.

p. 16 "Drew Brees: What They Say," JockBio.com, http://www.jockbio. com/Bios/Brees/Brees_they-say. html (accessed February 1, 2010).

p. 22 "Drew Brees: What They Say."

p. 26 Lee Jenkins, "His Eyes Wide Shut, Brees Saves Career," *New York Times*, 2005, http://www. nytimes.com/2005/01/07/ sports/07iht-chargers.html?_ r=4&pagewanted=1.

p. 28 "Drew Brees: What They Say."

p. 30 John DeShazier, "New Orleans Saints' Return to Superdome in 2006 Defines Franchise, Unless … ," Nola.com, January 23, 2010, http://www.nola.com/saints/ index.ssf/2010/01/new_orleans_ saints_return_to_s.html.

p. 33 "Brees Named Super Bowl MVP."

p. 34 Seth Wickersham, "Brees: Helping New Orleans is Rewarding Experience," ESPN, May 22, 2008, http://sports. espn.go.com/nfl/columns/ story?columnist=wickersham_ seth&id=3407718.

p. 35 Wickersham.

p. 36 Wickersham.

p. 37 "Drew Brees: What They Say."

p. 39 Simon Evans, "Proud Brees Savors Moment as New Orleans Celebrates," Reuters, January 25, 2010, http://www.reuters.com/ article/idUSTRE60O1CQ20100125.

True or False Answers

p. 7:   False. Super Bowl XLIV, in 2010, was Brees's first.

p. 12:   False. Brees is right-handed.

p. 20:   True.

p. 27:   False. In college, Brees wore number 15.

p. 31:   True.

p. 33:   False. Brees had been selected four times (2004, 2006, 2008, and 2009).

p. 38:   True.

Brees loves the challenge of being a quick-thinking and fast-acting quarterback.

Index

About the Author

Michael Portman has worked in the field of sports and recreation for over 15 years. He holds a degree in political science from Houghton College. He is an avid fan of football, baseball, and hockey, and enjoys attending professional and college sporting events. Michael lives and writes in Gainesville, Florida.